Earth and Moon

Torrey Maloof

Consultants

Sally Creel, Ed.D.
Curriculum Consultant

Leann Iacuone, M.A.T., NBCT, ATC
Riverside Unified School District

Jill Tobin
California Teacher of the Year
Semi-Finalist
Burbank Unified School District

Image Credits: p.2 Robert Matton AB/Alamy;
p.5 Zoonar GmbH/Alamy; p.13 Hillary Dunlap;
p.19 iStock; p.14 Amiko Kauderer/NASA; p.18 Glenn
Research Center/NASA; pp.20–21 (illustrations)
Chris Sabatino; all other images from Shutterstock.

Library of Congress Cataloging-in-Publication Data

Maloof, Torrey, author.
  Earth and Moon / Torrey Maloof; consultants, Sally
Creel, Ed.D. curriculum consultant, Leann Iacuone, M.A.T.,
NBCT, ATC Riverside Unified School District, Jill Tobin,
California Teacher of the Year Semi-Finalist, Burbank
Unified School District.
    pages cm
  Includes index.
  ISBN 978-1-4807-4571-1 (pbk.)
  ISBN 978-1-4807-5061-6 (ebook)
1. Earth (Planet)—Juvenile literature.
2. Moon—Juvenile literature. I. Title.
  QB631.4.M354 2015
  525—dc23
                                        2014013186

Teacher Created Materials
5301 Oceanus Drive
Huntington Beach, CA 92649-1030
http://www.tcmpub.com
ISBN 978-1-4807-4571-1
© 2015 Teacher Created Materials, Inc.
Made in China
Nordica.082015.CA21501181

Table of Contents

Our Home

We all live on Earth. Earth is a round **planet** in space that **rotates** (ROH-teytz), or spins. It also travels around a big bright star called the sun.

Earth is always moving.

Night and Day

You cannot feel it, but Earth is always moving. It takes 24 hours to make one full turn.

It is daytime in New York.

As it rotates, the part of Earth that faces the sun gets light and warmth. On that part of the planet, it is day.

Earth rotates on its axis just like a top.

Axis

Earth's Axis

Earth rotates on its **axis**. An axis is an imaginary line that Earth spins around.

At the same time, the other part of Earth faces away from the sun. On that part of Earth it is night.

day

night

It is daytime on one side of Earth.
It is nighttime on the other side.

As Earth rotates, night turns into day and day turns into night.

It is nighttime in China.

In the morning, the sun appears to rise. It rises in the east. The sun reaches its highest point in the afternoon.

morning

In the evening, the sun appears to sink in the sky. It sets in the west.

afternoon

evening

Goodnight, Moon

As the sun sets, the moon becomes easier to see in the sky. It does not always look the same. It changes every night!

Day or Night

We mainly see the moon at night. But sometimes we can see it during the day.

The moon changes because it travels around Earth. These changes are called **phases** (FEY-zez).

This shows the moon's phases.

The sun lights half the moon, just like it lights Earth. The other half of the moon is in darkness.

Here we can only see part of the lit side of the moon.

As the moon moves around Earth, we see part of the lit side.

Moon Walk

Only 12 people have walked on the moon.

About once a month, the entire sunlit side of the moon faces Earth. This phase is called a **full moon**.

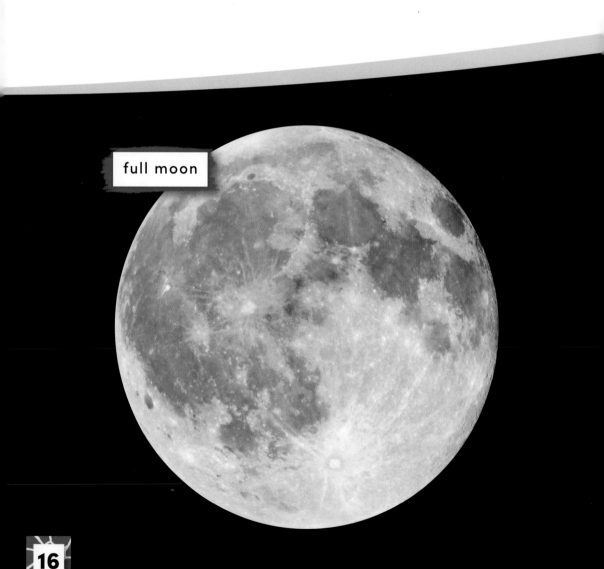

full moon

When the sunlit part is facing away from Earth, we cannot see the moon. This phase is called a **new moon**.

A new moon looks as though there is no moon in the sky.

new moon

On the Move!

Earth is constantly on the move. So is the moon! Because of all this movement, we have days and nights. We have different phases of the moon. And we have a special place to call home.

This is what Earth looks like from the moon.

Let's Do Science!

Why does the moon look different at times? Try this and see!

What to Get

○ ball

○ lamp

○ paper and pencil

What to Do

1 Pretend that the ball is the moon, your head is Earth, and the lamp is the sun. Put the lamp in the middle of the room with all other lights off.

2 Hold up the ball and move it in front of the light.

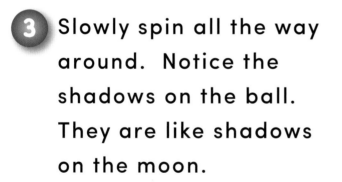

3 Slowly spin all the way around. Notice the shadows on the ball. They are like shadows on the moon.

4 Draw pictures of the shadows you saw. Look at your drawings. What do you notice?

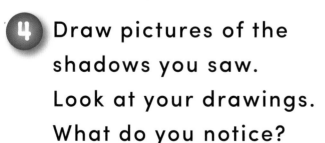

Glossary

axis—the imaginary line that Earth spins around

full moon—the moon when it looks like a complete bright circle

new moon—the moon when it looks completely dark

phases—the eight shapes of the lit side of the moon

planet—a large, round object in space that travels around a star

rotates—turns or spins

Index

Your Turn!

Phases of the Moon

Look for the moon each day. Draw its shape. Notice how it changes. How many phases can you see?